Exploring Materials

Glass

Abby Colich

Heinemann
LIBRARY
Chicago, Illinois

To contact Capstone Global Library please phone 800-747-4992, or
visit our website www.capstonepub.com

Edited by Abby Colich, Daniel Nunn, and Catherine Veitch
Designed by Marcus Bell
Picture research by Tracy Cummins
Production by Victoria Fitzgerald
Originated by Capstone Global Library Ltd
Printed in the United States of America in North Mankato, MN.
072013   007636RP

17 16 15 14 13
10 9 8 7 6 5 4 3 2

Library of Congress Cataloging-in-Publication Data
Colich, Abby.
  Glass / Abby Colich.
     pages cm.—(Exploring materials)
  Includes bibliographical references and index.
  ISBN 978-1-4329-8014-6 (hb)—ISBN 978-1-4329-8022-1 (pb) 1.
Glass—Juvenile literature. I. Title.

TP857.3.C54 2014
666'.1—dc23   2012047487

Acknowledgments
The author and publisher are grateful to the following for permission
to reproduce copyright material: Corbis pp. 9, 23b (© Marc
Romanelli/Blend Images); Getty Images pp. 10, 23c (© Philip and
Karen Smith), p19 (© Mark Williamson); Photo Researchers p. 8 (©
RIA Novosti/Science Source); Shutterstock pp. 4 (© Ingrid Maasik),
5 (© sritangphoto), 6a (© action studio), 6b (© Peter Hansen),
6c (© Sofiaworld), 6d (© lisasaadphotography), 7 (© Dudarev
Mikhail), 11 (© Tatiana Popova), 12 (© Tom Wang), 13 (© Ramon
grosso dolarea), 14 (© shadow216), 15 (© Galushko Sergey), 16
(© Tristanbm), 17 (© Diego Cervo), 18 (© Rostislav Glinsky), 20
(© Dhoxax), 21 (© LouLouPhotos), 22 (Anteromite, © akiyoko, ©
threeseven), 23a (© Diego Cervo).

Cover photograph of a schoolgirl looking through a magnifying
glass reproduced with permission of age fotostock
(© WAVEBREAKMEDIA LTD).
Back cover photograph reproduced with permission of Shutterstock
(© Ramon grosso dolarea).

We would like to thank Valarie Akerson, Nancy Harris, Dee Reid,
and Diana Bentley for their invaluable help in the preparation of
this book.

Every effort has been made to contact copyright holders of any
material reproduced in this book. Any omissions will be rectified in
subsequent printings if notice is given to the publisher.

Contents

What Is Glass?

Glass is a material.

Materials are what things are made from.

Glass has many uses.

We use glass to make many
different things.

Where Does Glass Come From?

Glass is made by people.

People melt sand and other materials together to make glass.

Glass can be recycled or reused.

Recycled glass can be used to make new things.

What Is Glass Like?

Glass can be clear.

Glass can be colored.

Glass is hard and smooth.

Glass can break. Broken glass
is sharp.

How Do We Use Glass?

We drink from glass cups.

container

We store food in glass containers.

Many windows are made of glass.

Some buildings are made of glass.

People wear glasses to help
them see.

People use glass to make art.

Quiz

Which of these things are made from glass?

Answer on page 24.

Picture Glossary

container something used to store things

melt when something becomes soft and runny as it is heated

recycle make used items into new things

Index

The **glass cups (a)** and **marbles (c)** are made from glass.

Notes for Parents and Teachers

Before reading

Ask children if they have heard the term "material" and what they think it means. Reinforce the concept of materials. Explain that all objects are made from different materials. A material is something that takes up space and can be used to make other things. Ask children to give examples of different materials. These may include glass, plastic, and metal.

To get children interested in the topic, ask if they know what glass is. Identify any misconceptions they may have. Ask them to think about whether their ideas might change as the book is read.

After reading

- Check to see if any of the identified misconceptions have changed.
- Show the children examples of glass, including marbles, glasses, and a drinking glass.
- Pass the glass objects around. Ask the children to describe the properties of each object. Is the glass colored or clear? Heavy or light? Ask them to name other items made from glass.